TREETOPS CLASSICS

FRANKENSTEIN

MARY SHELLEY
adapted by Nick Warburton

OXFORD
UNIVERSITY PRESS

OXFORD
UNIVERSITY PRESS

Great Clarendon Street, Oxford OX2 6DP

Oxford University Press is a department of the University of Oxford.
It furthers the University's objective of excellence in research, scholarship,
and education by publishing worldwide in

Oxford New York

Auckland Cape Town Dar es Salaam Hong Kong Karachi
Kuala Lumpur Madrid Melbourne Mexico City Nairobi
New Delhi Shanghai Taipei Toronto

With Offices in

Argentina Austria Brazil Chile Czech Republic France Greece
Guatemala Hungary Italy Japan South Korea Poland Portugal
Singapore Switzerland Thailand Turkey Ukraine Vietnam

Oxford is a registered trade mark of Oxford University Press
in the UK and in certain other countries

ISBN-13: 9-780199-1-93257
ISBN-10: 0-19-919325-8

Cover: Mark Edwards
Inside illustrations: Barry Wilkinson

Printed in Great Britain

About the Author

MARY SHELLEY

1797–1851

Frankenstein is probably the first 'mad scientist' story. Many films and books have been based on it or borrowed ideas from it.

The idea for the book came from a dream Mary Shelley had on holiday in Switzerland. She saw a man creating something in a laboratory, and it coming to life. She saw him run away from it in horror and go to bed; and then wake up terrified, with it staring at him.

The weather in Switzerland was so terrible that Mary and her friends decided to write horror stories. *Frankenstein* was the only story finished.

CHAPTER I

Captain Walton's Story

Figures on the Ice

We were journeying through the frozen waters of the north, in search of the Pole, when my ship became stuck fast in the ice. So there was nothing we could do but wait. I did not mind – I had always wanted to explore that strange, wild place of ice and mist. It seemed to me not just remote and lonely, but also very beautiful.

It was easy to imagine we were the only living creatures that close to the North Pole, so I was astonished, one bleak afternoon, to make out a tiny speck moving across the icy plain. The crew and I watched it closely and, as it drew nearer to the ship, we saw that it was a sledge pulled by dogs and guided by a huge figure. At first I supposed this figure to be human – what else could it be? – but when I was able to make out more detail I realized he was at least eight feet tall and quite unlike any man I had ever seen. We watched him plough on, northwards at incredible speed, until he vanished from sight. Who he was, or where he was going, we had no idea.

About two hours after this, the ice began to groan and crack, and our ship was freed. Some of the crew wanted to sail at once, but I was afraid we would be crushed by loose masses of floating ice. I ordered us to wait one night longer, and took the chance to get some sleep.

At first light I heard shouting on deck and went up to find the crew gathered at the ship's side. They were peering down at a man huddled against a sledge on a large raft of ice. This man was of ordinary size and quite clearly not the figure we had seen only hours before. How strange, I thought, to come across two souls within a few hours of each other, and in such a deserted place.

We hauled the stranger aboard, half dead with cold and hunger. I told the men to wrap him in blankets and warm him by the ship's stove. They were curious to know what he was doing alone in that desolate place – I was, too – but he was in no state to answer questions. So he rested there, barely able to move or speak, and two days passed before he was strong enough to respond.

Then he told me his name – Victor Frankenstein – and said he was a scientist. When I asked if his studies had brought him to the frozen north, he looked at me with a deep sadness.

'I have been searching,' he said slowly. 'Someone is trying to escape me, but he must be found.'

'Someone in a sledge, like yours?'

'Yes.'

'Then I think we've seen him. A day before we picked you up.'

On hearing this he became agitated and struggled to sit up.

'What is it?' I said, holding him by the shoulders. 'What's troubling you?'

At first he would not answer. He said his story was terrible, too terrible to hear. He said I would not believe him. But I could see that there was something desperate about him, that he wanted to tell me.

Eventually he calmed himself and began to speak.

CHAPTER 2

Frankenstein's Story

A Flash of Lightning

I am from Geneva, in Switzerland. My childhood there was a happy one: I knew nothing of the horrors waiting for me in later life. How could I?

To me the world was full of interest, and what fascinated me most was nature. I loved to read about it, to study it, to watch the plants and creatures around my home and wonder how they worked. My father used to laugh at this and say that I was more interested in nature than I was in people, but that was not entirely true. I did have friends and two in particular I truly loved. One was Henry Clerval, a boy of about my own age, and the other was my sister Elizabeth.

Elizabeth was not, in fact, a true sister; my parents had adopted her when I was five. I remember the day she came to us. My mother told me she had a present for me, and then, to my surprise, introduced me to this little blue-eyed girl.

'Here, Victor,' she said. 'This is your present – your new sister.'

I was delighted and somehow came to believe that Elizabeth really did belong to me, and that I was responsible for her. She was quite unlike me. While I was impatient and sometimes given to outbursts of temper, she was sweet-natured and generous. Over the years, I became devoted to her. My two little brothers, Ernest and William, loved her too. She came to be the very heart of that happy family.

One day, when I was about fifteen, a violent storm rumbled out of the mountains and broke over our home. I stood amazed at the door, listening to the crashes of thunder and blinking at the great flashes of lightning which lit up the garden. There was an old oak tree not very far from the house, and, as I watched, I saw it bathed in a sudden and immense stream of fire. When the light was gone, the tree was left a blasted stump, smoking in the rain.

It thrilled me to see such a thing, but I found the *idea* of it even more thrilling. I marvelled at the power and life there must be in all that electricity! If it could destroy such a huge, solid tree, I thought, what else might it do? If only it were possible to harness that power, what great things might be achieved?

From that moment I was determined to find the answers to these questions, to discover the secrets of life.

◆◆◆

The time came for me to go to university in Ingoldstadt. I was keen to go, but, just before I was to set out, my mother fell ill with a fever and died. Her parting wish was that Elizabeth would take her place and become a mother to Ernest and William, and that she and I would one day be married.

The house was filled with grief at my mother's death, and I could not abandon my family to go searching after knowledge in Ingoldstadt. I felt it was my duty to stay and comfort Elizabeth and my father in their sadness. In the end, of course, I had to leave, but my heart was heavy as I climbed into the coach that was to take me away. My father was there to give me his blessing, and Henry Clerval came to wish me good fortune. It was, I know, his fondest wish to come with me and join me in my studies, but his father would not allow it. My dear Elizabeth clasped my hands and begged me to write, to write often, and I promised that I would.

When I got to the university, however, I forgot my promise to Elizabeth. Ingoldstadt was a place of great learning, a place where I realized I could at last tackle the questions which had fascinated me for so long. I threw myself into my studies of the sciences and, over the next two years, barely wrote to my family and found no time to pay them a single visit.

During this time, I think I impressed my teachers with my enthusiasm for work and the speed of my progress. I recall hearing two of them talk about me as they walked through the cloisters one day.

'He's only been here two years,' one said, 'and I honestly believe he's learned everything we can possibly teach him.'

'Perhaps so,' said the other, 'but there's something secretive about the boy. I sometimes wonder where all these private studies will lead him.'

I smiled to hear this because I knew my understanding of science was not just the equal of theirs but far superior.

Yes, my studies were sometimes carried out in secret, but I felt sure that they were leading me to the brink of a remarkable discovery.

I used to work, alone and often deep into the night, in a little room at the top of the house where I lived. In fact, I drove myself so hard that I became quite ill – pale and wearied – though I hardly noticed it at the time. What concerned me was the same problem which had fascinated me as a boy – that of life itself. Where, I wondered, does it spring from? What is it that brings it about? I realized that, to find the answers to these questions, I had to examine not just living things but dead ones. I had to understand death and decay.

With this in mind, I took myself to churchyards during the most secret hours of darkness. There I saw how the power and vigour of the human form became mere food for worms.

In the bodies which I dug up I saw corruption and decay, and from this I gained a deeper knowledge of how things came to be alive. I toiled long and hard, ignoring what all this work was doing to my poor mind and body, and eventually I had my reward. Towards the end of one fateful night, I looked down at the dead flesh I had pinned to my workbench and I saw it move.

I had created life!

Now, looking back on all the dreadful things that were to come, I can only think of that discovery with horror. Then, however, it seemed to me to be a marvel, a triumph of my own brilliance.

CHAPTER 3

Frankenstein's Story

The Secret of Life

Oh, Walton, if only I had stopped there. I had succeeded in bringing dead matter back to life – surely that was enough. But no. I would not rest until I had taken my experiments as far as they would go. I wanted to create a living being, a creature like myself but perfect and original. I believed that this new creature would know I was its maker. It would bless me and be grateful.

So I returned to the graveyard, to the slaughter house and the dissecting room, and brought back to my lonely room the materials I needed – bone and flesh and muscle and arteries. Can you imagine the horror of all this? Dabbling in damp graves and torturing living animals to bring dead flesh to life? Oh yes, I was often appalled by what I was doing, but I could not stop. It was as if there were something inside driving me on.

I worked feverishly throughout that summer, becoming more and more weary in mind and body. Then, one dreary night in November, with the rain beating against my window, I stood back from my work and knew that it was almost done. On the bench before me lay a huge figure assembled from the gory fragments I had collected. All that was required now was the spark that would bring it to life, a flash of electricity like the one I'd seen destroy the tree. I worked on into the morning until, at last, that moment came.

There was a rush of air as its massive chest heaved. I saw its eyes open.

I felt a surge of triumph, but it lasted no more than an instant. Then I was overcome with a feeling of disgust. I had chosen parts from bodies that would make the creature beautiful, but it was nothing of the kind. The skin which covered its face was like dry, yellow paper. Its eyes were dull and its lips black and straight. I could not bear the sight of it. I ran from the room in horror and shut myself in my bedroom. There I paced about, asking myself: what have I done? What have I done?

Later that night, I woke from a restless sleep. My teeth were chattering and the sweat of fever made every limb shake. There at the foot of my bed was the monster I had created. It was standing in the moonlight, its eyes fixed on me and its jaw open in an evil grin. One hand was stretched out to me and from its throat came a harsh, unearthly sound. I did not wait to hear what it meant to say, or if it was capable of meaning at all. I pushed past it and hurried madly down the stairs – down, down and out into the cold night air of the town.

I wandered the streets, tormented by the failure of my dream and the horror of what I had done. It was light before I dared to return. I was about to climb the stairs to that dreadful room again when there was a knock at the door. Imagine my relief when I saw my old friend, Henry Clerval, on the doorstep.

'My dear Frankenstein,' he said, grasping my hand. 'Can you guess? Father has agreed at last. I am to study at the University!'

Then he looked into my eyes and his face clouded with worry.

'But, Victor, what's the matter?' he said. 'You don't look well.'

I assured him it was nothing – no more than the effects of hard work.

'Are you sure? Has something happened? You've written no letters, sent no news, and we've all been so worried about you . . . '

'Only because I've been so busy, Henry, I promise you,' I said. 'But my work is over now and I am free again.'

But was I free? Could I ever be free while that dreadful thing was waiting for me in my work room? I could not bear to think of Henry discovering my secret, so I asked him to wait awhile and I hurried up the stairs. I reached my door and hesitated, shuddering at the thought of what might still lurk behind it. Then I flung it open.

The room was empty. The monster had gone.

Henry Clerval was right, of course. The strain of all this *had* made me ill, and during the next few months I was confined to my bed. All this time Henry watched over me. I was too unwell to write home, so he wrote for me and then sat beside me to read the letters Elizabeth sent back. It was in one of these letters that I first heard about Justine. She was a girl my father had employed to look after my brothers. She was sweet-natured, Elizabeth wrote, and a great help to the whole family. Elizabeth's letters made me long to regain my strength so that I could go to see her. Long years had passed since I first parted from those I loved.

Henry's good company did much to restore my health, and, in time, I felt well enough to study again. However, I refused to have any more to do with my old work. Instead I joined Henry who was studying Oriental languages. My decision puzzled him.

'But why, Victor?' he asked. 'Surely you haven't lost your love of science?'

I told him I wanted to learn something new: I could not tell him my real reason.

As my health improved, I managed to push the dread of what I had done to the back of my mind, and I appeared, at least outwardly, to be happy and carefree.

Soon, I thought, soon I shall see my home again.

However, one day, when Henry and I were sharing breakfast, a letter came from my father, and the news it contained threw me back into despair.

'What on earth is it?' Henry asked anxiously.

'I must go back to Geneva immediately,' I said, almost overcome with grief. 'William is dead.'

'Dead? But he can't be . . . '

'He's dead, Henry! Read it yourself and see.'

My little brother had taken a walk one evening and not returned. The family had searched for him and found him at last, stretched out on the grass with the marks of some cruel hand on his neck.

At length Henry looked up from the letter, pale with shock.

'Murdered?' he whispered. 'I don't understand. He was such a sweet child, so innocent . . .'

'It's there in my father's own hand,' I said bitterly. 'William was wearing a locket. It bore a portrait of my mother, and when his body was found, the locket was missing. Clearly, he was murdered for it. And now Elizabeth blames herself because she gave him the locket. She weeps all the time and won't be comforted. Henry, will you help me to pack? I must go to them tonight.'

CHAPTER 4

Frankenstein's Story

The Locket

My carriage drove through the night and all was in thick darkness when I reached my home town. By then the city gates were locked so I was not able to go straight to the house. I therefore decided to walk out and see for myself the fateful spot where poor William had died.

As I walked, thunder rumbled in the mountains all around and rain began to fall in heavy drops. When I reached the place, the storm was at its fiercest and the countryside was lit up by wild flashes of lightning. With the rain streaming down my face, I clasped my hands together and looked up into the darkness. In my mind's eye I saw my little brother as I remembered him, so young and innocent, and the image filled me with unbearable sadness.

I thought I was alone with my grief but, suddenly, I caught sight of something stirring in the gloom. A figure darted from a clump of trees. There was another blaze of lightning. In its glare I saw quite clearly a vast and hideous shape lumber off into the dark, and I knew without a doubt that it was the monster I had created.

For a moment I was too stunned to move. I had not seen the creature for two years. What was it doing here, of all places? Then the truth dawned on me. Surely this vile thing was poor William's murderer. I had given life to the dreadful being that had killed my own brother.

In the next lightning flash I saw him again, clambering over a rock in the distance as he escaped into the mountains.

'What have I done?' I cried aloud. 'Oh, what have I let loose on the world?'

◆◆◆

As I made my way to my old home next morning, I knew I could say nothing of what I had seen. It was too terrible to speak of, and, anyway, how could they believe such a horrifying story?

I pushed open the familiar door and called for my father. My brother Ernest and my dear Elizabeth came running to greet me. She was more lovely than ever, but I could see at once the sadness in her eyes. My father looked much older than he was the last time I'd seen him. His face was lined with pain and dejection. In spite of this, he smiled to see me and shook me warmly by the hand.

'Thank heavens you've come, Victor,' he said. 'I'm afraid we have had more news of this tragic business, and it is even worse than we thought.'

Even worse? Had he, too, seen the monster? If so, he would surely soon learn of my part in William's murder. And how could I explain myself then? How could he ever forgive me when he knew the horrible truth?

'The locket has been found,' he went on. 'We now know who did this terrible thing.'

'Who?' I asked in a frightened voice. 'Tell me.'

'I can hardly bring myself to do so, Victor, for it is one of our own servants . . . '

'No!' I cried. 'I know that can't be true!'

'How can you know? There's no other explanation. It is Justine, the girl who came to help us with the children.'

'But it can't be. Elizabeth wrote to me about her. She said she loved my brothers . . . '

'So we all thought,' said my father, shaking his head sadly, 'but the locket was found among her things. She must have killed the child to get it. How else could she have come by it?'

I had no answer for this, yet in my heart I knew that Justine was innocent. I had seen my own creation at the scene of the crime, and I was certain that he alone was responsible for William's death. But how could I tell my father this? How could I explain to him that I had created my brother's murderer and released him into the world? All I could do was repeat that Justine must be innocent.

'I wish that were true, Victor,' my father said. 'Justine has always been faithful and very dear to all of us; why, she's like a member of the family. But she has the locket – I've seen it myself – and she cannot tell us how she came by it.'

'Then I must speak to her,' I said. 'I must do all that I can to help her.'

Elizabeth said she would come with me to visit Justine in her cell.

'I cannot believe that Justine took William's life,' she said as we made our way to the court. 'You will help her, won't you, Victor? You'll find out the truth?'

'I know she is innocent,' I told her, 'and you may be sure I shall prove it.'

Justine was pleased to see us and seemed calm enough, but it was clear to us that she was also frightened and bewildered. And it was just as clear that she had nothing to do with William's death. But she could tell us nothing that would help her case.

'I don't know how I came by the locket,' she said tearfully. 'I went to see my aunt on that night and the city gates were shut when I returned, so I had to take shelter in a barn.'

'You saw no one there?' I asked.

'No. As I slept I thought I heard footsteps, but I saw nothing.'

This was the story she told in court on the next day.

But everything depended on her possession of the locket, and she had no explanation for that.

The knowledge of my own part in this appalling business weighed heavily on me, and as the lawyers asked Justine question after question, and as the poor girl struggled to hold back her tears, I could stand it no longer and I rushed from the court.

There was nothing I could do to help.

Justine was found guilty of murder and condemned to death. This was shocking enough, but when Elizabeth and I called to see her for the last time, we heard that she had confessed.

'But why?' I asked. 'You know you are innocent.'

'A priest came to see me,' she said simply. 'He told me I would go to hell if I didn't confess.'

In the gloom of that damp cell, Elizabeth took hold of the poor girl's hands and squeezed them.

'I can't believe you would harm William,' she said.

'I didn't, miss!' she sobbed. 'I am innocent, I swear it!'

Then, turning to me, she said, 'Thank you, sir. Thank you for believing me.'

So she went to her death.

The injustice of this was torture to me. Now two innocent children were in their graves, and my family had suffered the most intense sorrow and desolation. And all of them were the victims of my hateful experiments.

◆◆◆

Although I was now back among the people I loved, I found it difficult to face them after the death of Justine. So I spent many long hours alone, brooding on thoughts of revenge and fearful that the monster might strike again. I knew how much I was to blame, and I was tortured by feelings of intense guilt. I suppose this seemed like simple sadness to the rest of the family, and perhaps that was why they avoided talking about what had happened. Elizabeth only spoke to me about it once, when we were out together in the carriage one afternoon.

She told me she was still convinced that Justine had been wrongly convicted and that the true culprit was still at large.

'I cannot understand why the villain who did this is free to walk wherever he likes,' she said. 'Oh Victor, why must men be like this? Why must they act like monsters, thirsting for each other's blood?'

She looked into my eyes as she said this and I think she must have seen something of my suffering there, for she took me by the hand and tried to calm me.

'Don't worry so,' she said softly. 'We have lived through terrible times but we have each other. Surely, that must give us hope. What can disturb our peace now?'

How could I answer her? How could I tell her that I feared for her life? I could not.

After that conversation, I found it even harder to speak to Elizabeth, and I took to wandering in the mountains on my own. And sometimes, when I gazed on the beauty of all I saw, I was able to forget myself a little. In time, I came to see that my presence in that sad house was only making matters worse, so I decided to leave. I told my father I would take a horse and ride into the Alps.

I rode for two whole days before stopping at a little place called Montavert. There I took a room at an inn, intending to be up early the next morning so that I could climb into the mountains, to be alone. There, at last, I might be able to think clearly.

The climb was long and difficult but I took no guide with me. I wanted solitude, not companionship, and the presence of a guide would do nothing to ease my restless mind.

All day I scrambled upwards, over crags and boulders and across a vast glacier, and I was weary and aching by the time I reached the summit. But what I saw there filled my soul with joy. A broad and lonely valley was spread out far below me, and beyond it loomed the immense and beautiful bulk of the great Mont Blanc. For the first time in weeks I felt something like happiness in my heart.

But the feeling was short-lived.

I was not alone, and only a moment later I saw a figure moving towards me over the glacier, moving with superhuman speed. It bounded easily over rocks I had struggled to climb.

I knew it, even at that distance. It was my own creature, the vile demon that had destroyed my family's happiness.

As soon as I recognized him, I was shaken by a fierce rage. I wanted to crush the life out of him and I did not care if I died in the attempt.

'Devil!' I cried as he approached. 'You dare to come to me after what you have done?'

He stared down at me out of his dull eyes but did not answer.

All at once I charged at him, burning with anger, but he brushed me aside with one sweep of his colossal arm. Then, for the first time, I heard him speak.

'Stay still and listen to me.'

'Why should I listen to a foul wretch like you?' I choked back at him.

'Oh, you are right, Frankenstein: I am a wretch. But who made me so? You did! You gave me life. You made me this miserable creature, hated by all men. It was your doing and you must listen to me!'

'You blame me for that?' I shouted. 'Then let me end it now! Let me put out the spark that created such a life of torment!'

'Listen to me,' he repeated. 'Listen or I will be the cause of more death and misery to those you love.' His anguished cry echoed over the valley. 'I was good and gentle when you made me. Cruelty taught me to be cruel. Now you have no choice, Frankenstein: you must hear my story.'

And I saw that, surely, he was right. If he lived in misery, it was because of me. However vile he was, he had the right to tell his story. So I suppressed my anger and prepared to listen. And this is what he said . . .

CHAPTER 5

The Monster's Story

I am Alive!

When I first awoke, I felt light and darkness against my eyes without understanding what they were. Sounds jumbled in my head and made no sense; my hands touched things I could not name. Everything was new to me – the whole world was strange and confusing. There was just one being – a creature something like myself – who might help me, and that was you. But when I turned to you, you fled from me in disgust.

I took some clothes – a few ill-fitting garments and a large cloak – and found my way outside. Then I left the dismal place of my creation far behind.

Now I know that it was night when I departed, but then I did not understand and the darkness frightened me.

I walked on until I came to a space where there were no buildings. Grass grew there and trees stood silently under a silver disc in the black sky. There I experienced fresh sensations. I discovered cold and hunger, and, by taking berries from the trees and shrubs, I learned what it was to eat.

After a while, I found the remains of a fire, left by some traveller, and saw first that it warmed me, and then that it filled me with pain when I tried to touch it. Thus, day by day, I travelled on, not knowing where I was going, and as I went I taught myself about the things that were good for me and the things that were harmful. I learned something about myself, also.

I came across people, other beings which I could see were almost like myself. Or so I thought at first. When I approached them, though, I found that they did not consider me as one of their own kind. As soon as they saw me, their faces became twisted with fear. They shouted at me and threw things and ran away from me, just as my own maker had done. So this is what I learned about myself – that I was a disgusting creature. Even though I had given them no cause, all men hated me.

Oh, Frankenstein, that was the hardest of all my lessons. How could I understand it?

I soon came to see that, to save myself from being beaten and chased and abused, I must stay out of sight. I had to live my life in secret, cowering and hiding and living on scraps. So I travelled on and eventually came across a cottage in the thick of the forest. It seemed a pleasant, tidy place, with a small garden in which there was a kind of rough shelter.

I shall stay here, I thought. I shall live in this hovel

of a shelter, and look out for the people who belong to this cottage. If I keep myself out of sight, perhaps I can learn from them.

◆◆◆

The first person I saw there was a girl who passed by my hovel carrying a pail of milk. I waited till she went into the cottage and then approached as silently as I could. I found a gap in the wooden shutters and watched her awhile through that. She was a pretty girl and I thought I could see kindness in her face as she busied herself, sweeping and tidying the cottage. I longed to speak to her, to make myself known and to hear her say gentle things to me, but, of course, I knew this was impossible. People did not say gentle things to creatures like me: they ran from me, or tried to beat me. So I remained hidden and watched.

Gradually I came to know the others who shared the cottage with the girl – a young man of about her age and an older man who seemed to be blind. It pleased me to see such attractive beings, going about their simple business. They were not altogether happy, though. I was puzzled to see that sometimes the young man and his companion would weep together.

Day by day I watched them closely and in that way learnt many things. I saw how people could live together in peace and love, and I also began to understand the

meanings of words and the way that language worked. I discovered the names they used for each other – the older man was 'father' or de Lacey, the other was Felix or sometimes 'brother', and the girl 'sister' or Agatha. They named the things around them – 'milk' and 'bread' and 'fire' – and they had books which they read together in the evenings.

If I can master their language, I thought, I can perhaps speak to them one day. And if they see that they have no need to fear me, then surely they will accept me and include me in their happiness.

My little family was not wealthy. Indeed, food and fuel were hard to come by, especially when the winds began to blow colder and the snows came. Felix and his sister sometimes went without food so that there was enough for the old man to eat. So I took to helping them in secret. I would collect wood for them to burn, and leave it near the cottage when they were away. It amazed them to come across my offering and they puzzled over where it might have come from. They were glad enough of it, though, and I felt so happy to see that my efforts brought them comfort.

When the spring came, I was surprised to see a visitor arrive at the cottage. She was a dark-haired, pretty girl named Safie. The whole family was delighted to see her, but Felix especially. So now I understood the reason why he had sometimes wept: he was in love with Safie and had been parted from her.

I watched and listened and so learned their story. Safie came from a distant land, a place called Turkey. It was there that she and Felix met and fell in love. They wanted to marry, but Safie's parents would not agree to it. At that time Turkey was at war with France and Safie's father was captured and thrown in prison. It was Felix who helped him to escape. When the French learned of this, they took all de Lacey's money and land, and the family had to flee for their lives. That was why they came to live in that poor cottage in the woods. When Safie found out where they were, she came to join them.

To begin with Safie found it hard to understand everything the others said to her. So Felix began to teach her. He explained the meanings of words and showed her books with stories in them. They studied like this every day and gradually Safie learned to speak and read.

I knew a little about books for I had found one in the pocket of your cloak. Of course, it meant nothing to me at first – just paper and strange marks – but as I followed Safie's lessons with Felix, I came to understand that the marks stood for words. I sat for many long hours with your book, struggling to make sense of it, and slowly it began to yield its meanings. They were your words, Frankenstein. The book was your diary and it told of your feelings as you set about the work you had started. You know it, Frankenstein – you know what you wrote.

'Oh, what am I doing by creating this monster? It is horrible, horrible!'

Can you imagine what I felt as these words became clear to me? My own master hated me. Can you imagine how I howled in anguish to the empty forest? But I had now seen other men and I knew they were not all like you. This happy family in the cottage was capable of love.

The thought that I too might speak to them and be happy one day filled me with hope, but it was a hope that did not last. While I was wandering alone in the forest, I came across a pool of still water, and knelt down to drink. There, suddenly, I saw my own face reflected and the sight of it made me shrink back in horror. This was the face my own creator despised. How could I, who was so hideous, ever speak to my secret friends, who were so graceful and lovely to look upon?

'What am I? What creature am I?' I cried aloud, but the only answers that came to me were my own groans of despair.

For a long time these thoughts tormented me and almost destroyed my dreams of companionship. I could not win friends because anyone who met me would recoil from my ugliness. I had no choice but to spend my life in hateful loneliness. Then, from out of this darkness I glimpsed a faint light of new hope and I realized that there might be a way after all. Mr de Lacey, the old man, was blind. He would feel no disgust or fear because he could not see me.

If I can only speak to him, I thought, he will not take me for a monster. He will only hear my voice. I will be able to tell him my story, and he will understand.

I was delighted with my plan. Once Mr de Lacey knew that there was some good in me, that I had helped his family and meant them no harm, he could persuade the others to accept me. So I waited for a day when Felix, Agatha and Safie were away from the cottage. Then, with my heart beating quickly, I went up to the door. I hesitated a moment, knowing that my future happiness depended on the next few minutes. I had to explain all that had happened to me, from beginning to end, and trust that this kind old man would then help to bring some comfort to my life.

I knocked on the door and, after a while, heard a voice call back.

CHAPTER 6

The Monster's Story

I Ask for Help

'Who is it? Who's there?'

'A traveller,' I answered. 'I am seeking rest and shelter.'

There was a brief silence and then the door was opened to me. Mr de Lacey stood before me, smiling warmly yet seeing nothing. I stepped into the cottage which I knew so well but had only seen by peering in at windows. The old man invited me to sit by the fire.

'Thank you,' I said. 'You are very kind.'

'Have you travelled far?' he asked. 'I can tell from your voice that you are not from this country.'

Indeed, my voice must have sounded strange to him – he was the first man I ever spoke to.

'Yes,' I told him. 'I am a stranger here, but I have friends nearby and I wish to make myself known to them.'

'Nearby? Where?'

'Close to this spot.'

'Then you will be with them soon, I hope. Who are they?'

I hesitated again before answering. Everything depended on his response to what I told him, and I was almost too afraid to continue. But I knew I had to speak.

'They are good, kind people,' I said, 'but they do not know me well. I fear that they might reject me before I can ask for their help.'

'If they are kind they will welcome you, surely. Why should they do otherwise?'

'Because I am so ugly to look upon. Men run from me before I can even speak to them.'

He listened carefully and nodded as I spoke. The room fell silent apart from the soft crackling of the fire.

'Well, my friend,' he said eventually, 'I am blind and cannot see you, but there is something in your voice that makes me trust you. Let me speak to your friends for you. I can tell them your story and prepare them.'

At this I became overwhelmed with happiness and fell to my knees. I clutched the good old man's hands.

'Oh, sir,' I cried, 'thank you, thank you. Those are the first kind words I ever heard. I knew you would help me . . .'

'You knew?' he said, a look of alarm on his face. 'How could you know? Who are you?'

'You and your family are the friends I spoke of, sir. I have seen you often. I have tried to help you . . .'

At that moment I heard the latch of the door click behind me. I turned and saw Felix, Safie and Agatha framed in the doorway, their faces frozen in shock.

'Father!' shouted Felix. 'What's going on? Who is this creature?'

It hurt me to see how Agatha hurried in to protect her father from me.

'Please,' I said, 'listen . . .'

But Felix had snatched up a branch from the pile by the fire. He swung it angrily at me. Again and again he beat me and I could neither resist him nor make him listen. I ran from the cottage, howling with frustration and fury, my hopes scattered and broken.

◆◆◆

I crawled back to my hovel and cowered there like a beast. The yellow skin of my wretched face was wet with tears. But as night came on, I became calmer and more able to reason. Surely, if I could make myself heard, if I could explain what I was trying to do, they would overcome their revulsion. However, when I crept back to the cottage, I saw the de Lacey family leaving, taking with them all that they could carry, and I knew that I had driven these gentle people from their home. They could not live in a place that harboured a monstrous creature such as me.

I watched them go, and then looked in at the window for the last time. It was so cold and empty now. A brief chance of happiness had been held out to me, and had then been dashed from my grasp. I felt rage build up inside me at the thought of this and suddenly I could bear it no longer. Fierce anger shook my body. I began to pile wood and kindling around the cottage, then I set fire to it and looked on as it roared and burned away to nothing.

And what could I do then, Frankenstein? Where could I turn for relief after being so cruelly denied? I knew of only one soul in the whole world who might help me. You – my maker, my creator!

So I left that place, too, and made my way to your home town – to Geneva.

◆◆◆

The journey was not an easy one. I was constantly reminded that mankind can feel only hatred for what it does not understand, that ugly creatures such as me can expect no sympathy. Even when I tried to do some good, men still shunned me. Once I saved a child from drowning in a river – and what was my reward? Her father snatched her from me, as if I were not her rescuer but the cause of danger. Then he turned a gun on me and shattered my flesh and bone. I sank to the ground, cursing all humanity and swearing vengeance on everyone I met from that day on. The pain of this wound was so great that I lost consciousness, but even as I fainted away there were still curses on my cracked lips.

Days of loneliness and pain followed before I was able to continue my journey, and two months passed before I eventually reached my destination. By then I was weary with travelling and sick at heart. Night was falling so I lay down to sleep in a field at the edge of the town. I do not know how long I remained there, but my sleep was a deep and soothing one, and it was only disturbed by the sounds of someone approaching. A little boy was coming towards me, a child so bright and innocent that, for a moment, the sight of him soothed the sickness in my heart. He seemed so young and natural that I thought there could be no taint of cruelty or evil in him.

If I can hold on to him a little while, I told myself, he will surely learn that I mean him no harm and come to know me as a friend.

But, as soon as he caught sight of me, he began the same old cries that I had heard throughout my life, from the very moment of my creation.

'Leave me alone! Monster! Ugly wretch!'

I held on to him and pleaded with him, but his cries grew more frantic.

'Monster, monster! I'll tell my father! He's a great man. His name is Frankenstein!'

The sound of that name cut me to my soul. Frankenstein! My enemy! I put my hands around his throat to stop his terrified screams, and before I knew what I had done his little body was lifeless at my feet. And when I saw that I had destroyed a thing my master must have loved, my heart was filled with bitter joy. I clapped my hands in triumph.

The child had a locket about his neck. I took it, not because I thought it was valuable, but simply because it was beautiful. Then I left him there for others to find, while I went in search of some better hiding place. I found it in the shape of an old barn. I thought this barn was empty, but when I went inside I saw a girl asleep on some straw. My mind was still full of murderous thoughts, and yet I hesitated to kill this sleeping girl. A better way of causing misery occurred to me. I hid the locket in the folds of her dress and crept away, knowing she would be blamed for the murder.

Oh, Frankenstein, you see how wild and bitter your creature has become! You see how I spread sorrow and heartbreak through the world! And why? Because I am alone and miserable. I have no friend or companion. And I shall be the cause of more sorrow and more deaths, unless you help me.

You alone can help me, Frankenstein. You must make a companion for me.

CHAPTER 7

Frankenstein's Story

The New Task

The monster stopped speaking. He was staring at me out of haunted eyes, waiting to hear my response, but I was shocked by his request. He wanted me to make him a mate. He was the cause of misery and death and he expected me to bring another such creature into the world. I could not – would not – do it.

'No!' I said firmly. 'It is impossible! Do what you like to me: I will never agree to it.'

He raged, as I expected him to, but then turned

his troubled face to me again and reasoned with me.

'It is because I am alone and hated that I have done these things,' he said in a low voice. 'If one single soul treated me with kindness, I would repay them with kindness. I would repay them over and over, and I would be at peace with the whole world. I know I can do great good, but not if I remain alone. Then I can only cause more and more destruction. Create a companion for me, Frankenstein, and you can prevent that.'

This argument made me pause and reconsider. It was true: I had created him and I was therefore responsible for his agony and suffering. If I took up my work again, and made a second creature, perhaps I *could* save countless other people from torment.

'Oh my creator, make me happy!' he added pitifully. 'Will you be that single soul who shows me kindness? Do not refuse me, master. Make me a companion. Then we shall go away together and be happy with each other, and neither you nor anyone else will ever see us again.'

'Very well, then,' I said. 'I shall do as you ask, but you must swear to keep your part of the bargain. If I create a mate for you, you will leave this place forever and never trouble humankind again.'

'I swear it,' he cried. 'By the sun and by the blue sky of Heaven, and by the fire of love that burns in my heart! Go home now and start your work. You will not see me again until it is finished.'

And with that he was gone.

◆◆◆

I returned to Geneva immediately.

At first I was determined to do all in my power to comply with the fiend's demands, but once I was back with my family I found it almost impossible to start. I feared the anger of the monster if I failed him, but the thought that I was to create another like him, as wild and as dangerous he was, weakened my resolve.

So I put off the task, and, whenever I was able to force the monster out of my mind, my heart was lighter and my health improved.

Then, after several weeks of inactivity, my father took me aside and said he had something which he wished to ask me.

There was anxiety in his face when he spoke, and I feared that he had learned the truth and was about to speak of the monster.

'You know I always hoped that you and Elizabeth would marry,' he said, looking steadily at me. 'Your own dear mother wished it, and I thought that you did too.'

'Of course I did, father,' I told him.

'But you have said no more about it. I can see how sad you are, Victor. Tell me, does this mean you have changed your mind? Is there someone else?'

'No,' I declared. 'How could there be? I can think of nothing that would please me more than marrying Elizabeth.'

And it was true. I was never more sure of anything.

'Then why have you not asked her?' he said simply.

The reason was clear enough to me: I could not marry Elizabeth while the threat of the monster remained hanging over me. I also knew that what I had to do could not be done in my father's house. Of course, I could not tell him this. Instead I said I had certain things I must attend to first, that I had to travel abroad again – to

England this time – and then I would return and marry Elizabeth.

On the morning I left, Elizabeth came to say goodbye. Seeing her there made me even more determined to put an end to this ugly business once and for all. Our happiness together was impossible until I had kept my dreadful promise to the monster.

My old friend Henry Clerval came with me. Henry was full of life and energy, and the idea of travel excited him. I took no pleasure in our journey, but he saw it as a wild adventure, a chance to see for himself places he had only read about. He did not know that I had chosen England because there was a scientist there who could help me with my appalling task.

We made our way to London. While Henry set off cheerfully to explore the city, I went to see this scientist and we talked about biology and anatomy. Naturally, I told him nothing about what I was planning to do, but I learned what I needed to know. At night I went out alone to collect the dreadful things I needed for my work. When all was ready, we set off on our travels again.

We journeyed north and crossed the border into Scotland. We took lodgings in Edinburgh and it was here that I finally told Henry that the last part of my journey had to be made alone.

'I am afraid I have some important work to do,' I told him, 'and I can put it off no longer. I need to find some remote island, some place where I know I will not be disturbed.'

'Ah well, my friend,' said Henry, 'if you must, you must. You go to your island and labour away in solitude, but I intend to make the best of our stay by touring this beautiful country.'

'Yes, good,' I said. 'And when this tiresome work is done, we shall meet again and then, I promise, I will be a much happier companion for you.'

So Henry set off and I found my island in the distant Orkneys, and arranged to transport all my boxes and equipment there by boat. The place was remote indeed – barren and stony with no more than three ramshackle huts on it – but it was well suited to the dreadful task ahead of me. I made one of these huts my laboratory and its simple table my work-bench, and set to work on my terrible assignment.

Once started, I worked hard, anxious to finish as soon as I could. I laboured throughout the hours of daylight, but I confess I was sickened and revolted by what I was doing.

When evening came I used to walk alone along the rocky shore and think of my home in Switzerland and especially of Elizabeth. I had seen nothing of the monster since that day in the Alps. Was he still there, in Geneva, hiding in shadows and watching her? These thoughts, and the foul work I was engaged on, made me uneasy. He would be with me, he said, when my work was done. Had he followed me to this remote island, I wondered? Was he lurking close at hand and watching me, even now?

The work progressed, in spite of these feelings, and gradually a second monster began to take shape. One evening, when the sun had set and a silver moon had risen above the sea, and it was too gloomy to continue, I sat deep in thought at the make-shift bench in my little hut.

I was thinking about the promise I had made to the monster, and the promise he had made to me. He said he would trouble me no more, and perhaps he intended to keep his word. But this new, still lifeless creature had made no such promise. I could not know what she would be like. Perhaps she would be a thousand times more vile than him and delight in murder and wretchedness. As these thoughts turned over and over in my mind, I glanced up at the window and saw there a dark shape silvered by moonlight.

It was the demon himself, staring in at me and grinning with malice!

Shock and fear ran through my body at the sight. He *had* followed me, as close and secret as a shadow, and now he was waiting for me to put the final touch of life into another like himself. Another like himself! I saw evil in his hideous face and the very idea disgusted me. Surely it was madness to create another malignant thing like him!

Immediately I jumped to my feet and began to destroy my new creation. In a frenzy I tore it apart while the monster watched. I saw him lift his head and heard him howl with rage. I looked down at the work I had ruined, and when I turned to the window again he had gone.

Then I was alone. Darkness descended and I sat in that bleak hut, staring out at the sea.

There was nothing I could do but wait and tremble, and dread the monster's return. And I was certain that he would return.

I do not know how long I sat there helplessly waiting, but eventually I heard the door flung open as he rushed into the hut.

'Why?' I heard him say in a voice low with menace. 'Why did you destroy what you created? Why did you break your promise?'

'I had no choice,' I answered shakily. 'I refuse to bring more misery into the world.'

'All men may have a wife,' he said. 'All beasts may have a mate. Why must I be alone? Do you think I can be content to see you happy while I am miserable because of you? No! I shall have my revenge on you, Frankenstein!'

'Leave me alone!' I cried.

'Yes, I will go now, but remember this: I shall be with you on your wedding night!'

On hearing this I made a grab at him but he escaped me with ease and moments later I saw his boat surge across the sea with unnatural speed. I stood on the stony beach and his words rang through my head – *I shall be with you on your wedding night!*

So – he had chosen the hour of my death. Part of me did not care: by this time I was so sickened by the whole business that I would have been glad to be rid of it all, to find peace at last, even through death.

It was only when I thought of the distress this would cause Elizabeth that I determined to live. And not only to live – I would make myself ready for the monster and fight him until he had wrung the last breath from my body.

When morning came, I decided to leave the island for good, to meet with Henry again and then return to Geneva.

Before doing so, however, I had one final task to perform. I packed up all my instruments and the remains of the female monster in baskets and loaded them into my little skiff.

Then I rowed away from the island, across a flat sea and under a placid sky.

When I felt I was as far from human eyes as I could get, I dropped the baskets over the side. As they gurgled

and sank out of sight, a feeling of weariness and great relief came over me. I stretched out in the bottom of the boat and fell into a deep sleep.

I woke hours later, with the sun low in the sky, the little boat tossing on angry waves and the island no longer in sight. I was shocked to see that I had been swept into the wide Atlantic Ocean – no sign of land, no sign of help – and that the wind was still forcing me on. There was nothing I could do but drive before this wind and hope to find land before I died of hunger and thirst. Darkness came and went, and the wind eased to a fresh breeze, but by then I was sick and weary, with hardly strength enough to hold on to the oars.

Then a line of cliffs appeared on the distant horizon and I dared to hope that I might be saved. Slowly, slowly, I drew closer and eventually I made out first a tiny cluster of buildings, and then a stony beach.

A group of people had gathered on the beach to watch me steer my boat in, but not one of them lifted a finger to help me, even when I fell as I tried to pull the boat onto the beach. This, and the way they huddled together and whispered, seemed strange.

'My friends,' I said, 'will you tell me the name of this place and where I can find shelter?'

There was a moment's silence, and then one of them stepped forward and spoke in a rough voice.

'This is Ireland, sir,' he said. 'And as to shelter, we have a jail in the town that will hold you fast enough.'

'A jail? But why?'

He gave me a look of the deepest suspicion. 'A man was found murdered here the night before last,' he said, 'and you must tell the magistrate what you know about it.'

CHAPTER 8

Frankenstein's Story

Close to Death

The magistrate was a mild-mannered old gentleman named Kirwin. I think he felt pity for me, and was half inclined to believe that I was innocent, but the evidence against me seemed overwhelming. He told me how some of the men, returning from a fishing trip, had stumbled on the body of a young man on the shore. He had been dead only a short while. His clothes were not wet and the only signs of violence to his body were the black marks of fingers about his neck.

Up to that point I had remained calm, insisting that there had been some misunderstanding which I could easily explain, but at the mention of those marks, I began to shake and I was barely able to stand. Black marks about the neck! I knew only too well what that must mean – the monster had struck again.

'So you *do* know something of this business,' said Mr Kirwin, watching me closely.

I struggled to control my feelings and look him in the eye. 'How can I?' I said. 'I never even saw this place until the storm drove me here.'

'Well, we shall see about that,' he said and he turned to make a signal to some of the men. 'Take him into the other room and show him the body.'

They took hold of me and led me into an ill-lit room where the corpse lay. I was still reeling at the news that the poor man had died at the monster's hand, but I remained perfectly certain that I could prove I was nowhere near at the time of death. I approached the coffin and looked in. What I saw there made me gasp for breath and cry out loud. Stretched out before me was the lifeless form of Henry Clerval.

'Henry!' I cried. 'My dear friend Henry!'

A murmur ran through the crowd when they heard this. I fell on the limp body of my dear companion and began to sob. 'Oh, my friend, have I been the cause of your death too?'

They were sure then that I knew the murdered man, and that I had condemned myself with my own words. It was all the proof they needed. I was dragged from the room, beside myself with grief, and thrown into a cell.

The shock of Henry's death took a heavy toll and I was plunged into such a burning fever that I lost all knowledge of where I was or what was happening to me. I lay on a wretched bed in that cell, shuddering in an agony of torment and crying out in a way which bewildered my captors. They heard me raving that first William and Justine and then my dearest friend had all been murdered because of me. All this, of course, made them even more convinced of my guilt.

The fever took me to the very brink of death, and though I did not die, I often wish I had. However, when I finally passed out of this nightmare, I opened my eyes to see Mr Kirwin standing over me.

'I am glad to see you recovered at last,' he said softly. 'You have been very ill.'

'How long have I been here?' I asked.

'Two months. Now, if you feel well enough, there is someone here who wishes to see you.'

His words were meant to comfort me, I know, but they only brought me more torture, for I felt sure this visitor was none other than the monster himself, come to gloat over me and mock.

'Keep him out of here!' I cried, twisting away from Mr Kirwin and covering my eyes. 'For God's sake, don't let him in!'

'Calm yourself, sir,' he said. 'Surely you will want to see your own father.'

I turned back to him immediately and sure enough there was my father standing behind him. My own dear father! So the creature had not come for me after all. Feeling almost overcome with relief, I lifted myself from the cot and stretched out my hand to him.

'You are still safe, then?' I said.

'Of course I am,' he told me, taking my hand. 'Why should I not be?'

'And Elizabeth, and Ernest?' I asked. 'There has been . . . no danger?'

'Not to us. But to you, my son . . . Oh, Victor, this is a sorry place for you to be. You travel to find happiness but wherever you go you are dogged by ill-fortune.'

'My fortune will improve now, father,' I said with a weak smile. 'Now that we are together again, everything is sure to be better.'

And it is true that, from then on, I began to regain my old strength. With my father's help I was able to answer the charges against me and prove that I was nowhere near the scene when poor Henry was murdered. Thus I was released from captivity. But, although I was fit and well again, my mind was far from easy. I could not forget the monster's vile promise, and I knew I had to return to Geneva, to watch over my family and to keep them safe.

◆◆◆

What pleased me most was that I was able to see Elizabeth again. In spite of this, however, I was unable to hide my fears from her. She did not know what caused them, but she could see clearly enough that I was troubled with dark thoughts. She thought that I had doubts about our marriage, and tried to reassure me.

'If there is someone else, Victor,' she said to me one day, 'you must not be afraid to tell me. I only want your happiness.'

'There is no one else, nor ever will be,' I told her. 'It is true that I have been afflicted by a terrible sadness, but I know that only you can help to soothe it. We will be married, I promise you. And then I will tell you the story of my misery. Until then, I beg you, do not ask me to speak of it.'

There were tears in her eyes as she listened to me, but she swore she would ask me no more questions, and the day we were to be married was fixed. That should have been a time of hope for both of us, but as it drew nearer the monster's words came back to haunt me. *I shall be with you on your wedding night.* I did all that I could to prepare myself to confront him. I carried pistols with me wherever I went and tried always to remain alert.

On our wedding day all seemed outwardly happy and carefree, and I tried to suppress these secret fears. A party of friends and family gathered to see us off as we set out to spend the first part of our new life together in Italy. That night we broke our journey on the shores of Lake Geneva where we found lodgings at an inn.

The day had been calm but as darkness descended a violent wind rose in the west and blew ominous clouds across the face of the moon. As the rain began to fall, I became more and more anxious. I could not sit still, I could not rest, and every moving shadow struck fear into my heart. The slightest sound would make me snatch up the pistols.

'Victor, what is it?' Elizabeth asked. 'What's the matter?'

'Something terrible,' I said distractedly. 'There is something terrible about this night.'

Then, when I looked at her, I saw my own fear reflected in her face and tried to comfort her.

'Peace, peace,' I said. 'Do not worry. I will see that we are safe enough.'

I knew what I had to face, but I did not want Elizabeth to face it too, so I told her to stay in our room while I went out to make sure all was well. For an hour I paced about the corridors, looking in every corner where the beast might be hiding. I found no trace of him.

I was about to return when I heard a piercing scream. A pause, and then another.

It came from our room. A sudden dreadful realization rushed into my mind. It was not me he sought – but Elizabeth! I stood there a moment, in frozen terror, and then rushed back to the room. Flinging open the door I saw her there, thrown across the bed, her head hanging down, her pale face half covered by her hair. The murderous marks of the fiend's hands were on her neck.

A faint sound made me look up at the open window. A hideous figure was crouching there. He was pointing at the lifeless form of Elizabeth, a grin twisted on his vile face.

I raised my pistol and fired at him but he was gone in an instant. I dashed to the window in time to see him plunge headlong into the lake.

◆◆◆

The news of Elizabeth's death was more than my poor father could bear. It broke his heart and he died in

my arms a few short days after I returned home. And me? All that was left for me was hatred of my own creation. I went alone to visit the graves of his victims, all those dearest to my heart, and I stood there in silent grief.

Lost – all love and happiness lost to me. Then rage replaced grief and I swore to pursue the creature to the ends of the earth. I swore out loud, kneeling on the grass to kiss the earth of their graves.

'Let the hellish monster feel the agony I feel now! Let him suffer my torment!'

There was a moment's silence and then I heard his fiendish laugh and knew he was nearby, watching me and mocking. His words came to me as close as a whisper.

'I am satisfied, Frankenstein. Miserable wretch, I am satisfied.'

I darted towards the sound but it was hopeless. He had what he wanted and left me alone.

Ever since then, my life has been spent in pursuit of him. Nothing else matters to me now. I must find him and destroy him. I have followed him through Europe and across the wilds of Russia, and always, always he has escaped me. Now, in this waste of ice and snow, I have come close to him only to lose him again.

CHAPTER 9

Captain Walton's Story

How it Ended

When Victor Frankenstein had finished his story, I could see that he did not have much longer to live. This terrible quest of his had driven him to exhaustion and he was doomed to spend his last days on an ice-bound ship, desolate and far from home.

'Walton, my friend,' he said to me as death closed in on him, 'if you should chance to see the monster again, you must promise that you will do all in your power to kill him. You have heard my story. You know he must not be allowed to live.'

With that he clasped my hand, and died.

He was a great man, and, I believe that but for these tragic events he could have been greater. I left him in peace, and prayed that it would be a true peace. When I returned to the cabin a little while later, however, I was confronted by a sight that I shall never forget. A huge, distorted shape loomed over the body of my poor dead friend. The creature's vast head was bowed and ragged hair hung down over his face.

And he was weeping.

He turned to look at me. I saw the deathly pale flesh of his parched face and recoiled in horror, but he was not concerned with me. He gazed back at the body of his creator.

'Oh, Frankenstein,' he said, 'forgive me, forgive me! I have murdered the lovely and the helpless. My wretched heart is breaking because of the innocent beings I destroyed. Now I have driven my own maker to his death. I am alone, more alone than ever.'

He choked over his own words, then turned sharply to me again and looked at me with dead and ugly eyes.

'You need not fear me,' he said quietly. 'Wherever I have gone I have been met with hatred. Now I have destroyed my greatest enemy – and my greatest friend – and all the hatred I have left is for myself.'

I watched in horror as he shambled to the cabin window, a pitiful and a broken figure.

'I shall leave now,' he said. 'My death awaits me. I shall build a fire that will consume my foul body and burn away all this misery. And then, pray God, my spirit will sleep in peace.'

Then he gave me one last look, leapt from the window and jumped down to his raft below. I looked down after him and saw him carried slowly away by the waves until he was lost in darkness and distance.